Why the Wait?

Why the Wait?

Kizzy Moraldo

RESOURCE *Publications* • Eugene, Oregon

WHY THE WAIT?

Copyright © 2022 Kizzy Moraldo. All rights reserved. Except for brief quotations in critical publications or reviews, no part of this book may be reproduced in any manner without prior written permission from the publisher. Write: Permissions, Wipf and Stock Publishers, 199 W. 8th Ave., Suite 3, Eugene, OR 97401.

Resource Publications
An Imprint of Wipf and Stock Publishers
199 W. 8th Ave., Suite 3
Eugene, OR 97401

www.wipfandstock.com

PAPERBACK ISBN: 978-1-6667-3164-4
HARDCOVER ISBN: 978-1-6667-2432-5
EBOOK ISBN: 978-1-6667-2433-2

MARCH 8, 2022 8:23 AM

Dedicated To:

Sterling and Halyn Moraldo
The page in my life turned, when you both entered in.
I love you both!

Frank and Belen Luna
Your commitment, sacrifice and love for Christ
has inspired me to do, what I thought I couldn't.

Sydney Luna
You unknowingly taught me about love,
years before I would become a mom.

Ileana Matos
We've shared so much over the years, thank you for being there.

Amanda Freitag and Sarah Edwards
Thank you both for your prayers and the many years
of dreams shared!

Contents

Chapter 1
PROLOGUE | 1

Chapter 2
THE WAITING OVERVIEW | 3

Chapter 3
LOOKING BACK | 7

Chapter 4
WANTING SPIRITUALITY | 12

Chapter 5
EARLY YEARS ON MY OWN | 14

Chapter 6
SALVATION | 21

Chapter 7
CALL FOR MY LIFE | 29

Chapter 8
MOVING ON | 40

Chapter 9
TURNING THIRTY | 40

Chapter 10
PASSING OF TIME | 44

Chapter 11
THE PAGES WILL TURN | 53

Chapter 12
DEALING WITH LONELINESS | 62

Chapter 13
UNDERSTANDING GOD'S PLAN | 68

Chapter 1

Prologue

I never thought that I would reach the ripe "old" age of forty-four and still be single. I always thought that marriage, family, and all of the things in life like that would eventually just fall into place. I never thought of what would happen if it didn't. Would I still live with a total commitment to my relationship with Christ? It can be easy to just think, "Yes! Of course! Nothing will stand in my way of a relationship with the living God." But what happens when decades pass? This is exactly what I have faced and had to answer for myself.

At twenty-one, life changed for me. I went from just wanting to be in a relationship to desiring marriage. I wanted to live for Christ, and I had a desperate desire to be a missionary overseas. All around me, the young people at my church and our surrounding sister churches began dating and heading toward marriage, most with that same desire to do big things for God. I remember thinking that my turn will come sooner or later. A couple of years after I became a Christian, one of my really good friends—who had been single a long time—came over and showed off her wedding album. After years of waiting, she had started dating at twenty-eight and finally got married at twenty-nine. She was overjoyed as she showed off her beautiful wedding pictures and gushed about how amazing her husband was. She said something that day I would always remember: "Kizzy, it was worth the wait." That day, I thought to myself, Well I hope I don't have to wait that long! Over the years, I have thought about that statement often. Never in my thoughts of the future or best laid plans did I ever think so many years would pass and I'd still be single . . . Why the wait?

I have also thought about all the "whys" and what-ifs, all of the things I could have done differently that perhaps may have changed my situation. But the thing I think of most often is, how do people deal with waiting to be married and the passing of time in the world we live in now? Perhaps the question isn't "Why the wait?" but "What is God's plan in the wait?" Of course, the plan is never laid out in detail before us, but as the story of our lives unfolds, so does God's plan. My life story has many facets to it. To tell all would require nothing short of a mini-series. But as I walk through parts of it—growing up, leaving home, coming to Christ, turning thirty, starting a family, and dealing with loneliness, I hope to encourage, inspire, and ultimately bring hope to you.

Chapter 2

The Waiting Overview

I haven't so much as been on a date in almost twenty years. I never thought I would be single at this point in life, and I know I'm not alone. This seems unbelievable when you talk about it with people, especially in this day and age of connection. We see an abundance of advertisements for dating apps that promises you will find "the one" regardless of preference, where you live, or even affiliations. Some even offer moneyback guarantees that you will find true love. Over the years, I have watched almost all of my friends get married, start families, purchase homes, and make major life decisions together while I've waited. I have watched these couples step into ministry in our churches, becoming pastors or missionaries, while I've waited. I have watched my own family members get married, have kids, and now those kids are all grown up and heading off to college while I've waited. In my early

Why the Wait?

twenties, my coworkers, friends, family, and even strangers would inevitably ask during the course of any conversation if I was seeing anyone. When I informed them that I wasn't, they would say things like, "You're young! There's no rush!" or "The right person will come along. You'll see!" or "Stop being impatient!" But as I have gotten older the questions and comments have gotten bolder and almost accusatory at times... "Don't you want to get married?" I have been asked many times. "You can't just sit there and just expect someone to appear. You have to do something." "What is it that you're looking for?" Or my favorite, "Maybe your standards are just too high." When I turned forty, I stepped over an invisible line where comments became that of resignation.

"Well not everyone is going to be married." "Being single means you're just free to focus on God." Even, "Consider yourself lucky. Marriage isn't all it's cracked up to be." And while there are truths in all of these statements, I've never felt like it satisfied the reason that I was still single. In the early days, as I watched all of my friends' lives take off, I wasn't bothered. I used to think to myself, Well, my turn is coming. I had a list of things I was praying for in a husband, and I would reference this list from time to time and just keep praying. I was involved in the church I was attending and at times so busy with work and all sorts of extra activities that I really didn't dwell on being single. When I entered my thirties, I was so happy to reach that point, I felt like I had matured and was ready for the next step in my life. But even though I felt like I was ready, I waited still. After a few years, I began to realize perhaps marriage was still going to be a little ways off, and I needed to just live. I could just sit around waiting for this person to just appear and be consumed with that, or I could live my life. Why did I feel like I needed to wait for someone to do some of the things that were personal

The Waiting Overview

goals of mine? I didn't give up praying for a husband, but I realized that I needed to consider what I was doing with myself.

When I had the opportunity to go back to college, I did. A few years later, I had an opportunity to purchase a home, and I did. I had the opportunity to do some traveling, go on a cruise, and just be available for things. I would be lying if I said that I have wanted to be single for this long. I think, like most people, there is a natural desire for companionship, a desire to talk to someone on a more intimate level than our best friend. To have a shoulder to lean on or be hugged and told we look beautiful as a woman, even on our worst days. As a mom, it's nice to think that perhaps I could have help around the house, especially when I'm sick and can't get out of bed to get the kids ready for school, make breakfast, pack lunches, school drop-offs, or make major decisions with regards to their well-being, educational needs, or just life in general. It's nice to think of having support in all of that, although you can be married and still wish for this kind of support. But as a Christian, I believe that God created the sanctity of marriage and it shouldn't be taken lightly. This is seen right from the beginning of the Bible in Genesis during the process of creation. God says, "It is not good that man should be left alone; I will make him a helper comparable to him" (Genesis 2:18, NKJV). In Genesis 2:24-25, it states, "Therefore a man shall leave his father and mother and be joined to his wife, and they shall become one flesh, and they were both naked, the man and his wife, and were not ashamed" (NKJV).

From there, we see the documentation of many marriages and families after Adam and Eve: the choosing of a wife for Isaac, the love story of Ruth, who ended up in the lineage of Christ through the good choices she made leading to her marriage to Boaz. Esther became queen after she was chosen to marry the King of Persia through divine intervention; this marriage was critical as Esther gained favor with the King, ultimately saving her people, the Jews, from genocide. The Bible provides many other examples of marriages, good and bad. So, with all this in mind, we can conclude that marriage is important to God. Who we marry is also important. What about when we marry? Some people seem to find their "soulmate" and get married very early on in their life, and for others, like myself it's not the case. I have often wondered, Should I be doing something to move this along other than just waiting? Am I doing something wrong? What purpose does all of this serve? Does God not see that I'm lonely, that I sometimes watch couples and think to myself, I want that? Now, we know there are no perfect couples, but in the mind of a single person, sometimes we think every relationship we see is perfect simply because they are in one and we're not. We have a way as human beings of seeing things through shaded lenses. I have pondered all of these questions over the years and for the longest time I was convinced that somewhere along the line I had missed the boat. I must have missed my chance at finding Mr. Right. But did I?

Chapter 3

Looking Back

Jeremiah 29:11 (ESV) "For I know the thoughts that I think towards you, says the LORD, thoughts of peace and not of evil, to give you a future and a hope."

Growing up, I had the plans for my life all mapped out. I did really well academically without much effort, and I thought education was my ticket to the life I wanted to live. I wanted to become a doctor and get far away from the inner-city life in Boston where I grew up. This goal consumed me. I really never thought about marriage or having a family, but I did want a boyfriend—someone to date and just hang out with, but not anything deeper than that.

At twenty-one, I became a born-again Christian and for the first time in my life, I began to see the beauty in family, marriage, and relationships. I came from a pretty dysfunctional household where we rarely did anything together as a family, so my perspective on family life was pretty skewed. In the house I grew up in, there were two married couples. One couple was my mom's parents. They immigrated from Trinidad and Tobago in their thirties, then moved around a little bit before finally settling down and purchasing a two-family home in Boston. Over a number of years, all of their nine children, some of whom were adults with children, all followed suit and came to America, eventually moving into that two-family home.

Although my grandparents worked hard, my grandfather had a major drinking problem. By the time my mom, who had recently separated from my dad, and my two other siblings moved into my grandparents' home, he had become a ragingly abusive alcoholic. I have very few memories of him sober.

The other married couple living with us was my mom's oldest sister. My aunt and her husband were workaholics. I hardly ever saw my uncle, and when I did see him, we never had a conversation further than "Hi, how are you?" They had a son who was the oldest teen in the house, and he ran the streets with his friends, got caught up in the life of drugs, alcohol, partying, and hanging out in the neighborhood by day and an addiction to pornography by night, which led to many deviant activities in the house. I never saw the three of them ever have a meal together, do any kind of family activity, or even sit and have a conversation with each other the entire time I lived in the house, which spanned roughly ten years.

Needless to say, we lived in a packed house. At one point, twenty-two of us lived in that house. I became close with one of my cousins who was two years younger. We spent a lot of those years in the house getting into all sorts of trouble. We were always in fights and hanging out in our neighborhood.

In a home where three generations of family lived, everyone was basically doing their own thing. I was seemingly always looking for acceptance and love. It was something I really didn't realize at the time; it was masked by a nonchalant attitude toward life and what was going on around me.

In middle school, my focus was on urban survival basically. I was constantly being bullied in school for looking nerdy. I wore these pink plastic glasses, my hair was never in the "right" styles, and all I wore were my best hand-me-downs from my sister. Upon entering high school, I began to notice (and was attracted to) the opposite sex for the first time. I remember being shocked on the first day of ninth grade when a classmate showed up heavily pregnant. I became aware of the heavy flirtations and interactions between a lot of the girls with the boys. It seemed like love was in the air as the boys were happy to oblige. I often wondered what all that attention would be like, as I definitely was not one of the popular girls and didn't hang around with the "in" crowd. To the contrary, no one paid much attention to me, and at times I felt a bit invisible.

My sophomore year of high school, marked a turning point in my life. One of my aunts in the house met a man that owned a hair salon in Boston with his siblings. They started dating. My aunt eventually moved out of our house, but would always come around with her new boyfriend. He seemed so different to our neat, West-Indian family because he was from Georgia and spoke with a strong southern accent. A lot of people in my family would talk about him behind his back as half couldn't understand him.

After they had married, I would frequent his salon as he would do my hair. At the time, my hair was really long, and I felt pretty for having long hair—I was trying to fit in with the popular girls at school, but still, no one seemed to pay much

Why the Wait?

attention to my changing appearance. One afternoon while visiting my aunt at her boyfriend's salon after school, I somehow ended up by myself with my uncle in their apartment. I didn't think anything of it. He was always so nice, but something was different that day. Being so naïve, I didn't pick up on the way he was speaking to me that afternoon. I can still remember the button-down red dress I was wearing that day as he came towards me in their little apartment and began to unbutton my dress. As he did this, he began to put his hands and mouth all over my body. I was paralyzed with fear. He was much bigger and stronger than me, and I can still remember the look in his eyes and face as he was touching me. I just felt numb and helpless. I went back home that night and began to feel so disgusted with myself.

He did this on a couple of other occasions—one time right at my house as my mom and aunt were talking in another part of the house, his hands down my shirt touching me. I began to hate myself, and constantly felt angry and violated. My mom was unapproachable, and I felt like I could not speak to anyone in my family about what had happened. I kept this secret all to myself and it ate me up inside. I became an angry individual, and I found myself not really caring about life. Growing up in the inner city, where violence abounded, I lost the fear I always had in the streets. I fought the bullies with an intention to harm. I just didn't care what happened to me any longer.

I got suspended from school in eleventh grade as, on one occasion, my anger turned to rage and I disrupted one of my classes to beat up a girl who felt the need to pick on me that day. During that fight, I picked up an object to strike her down before I was restrained and sent home. I felt alone and frustrated but held on to the hope of leaving my house one day to pursue my life away from all the drama. I was no longer interested in trying to get the boys in school to notice me, and popularity lost its appeal as I became more withdrawn.

Chapter 4

Wanting Spirituality

During this time, my mom and my siblings went to many different churches in and around where we lived. After my mom met a local pastor at one of her community college classes, she quickly settled into this particular church and became involved with it. In addition to her search for a church, my mom would wake us up every morning at the crack of dawn to read us chapters from the Bible. After reading the selected chapter, she would explain it to us by reading from an extensive commentary she had. It was overwhelming to say the least, and very little of what she was reading was understood by any of us outside of the typical Bible stories we all probably know—the ten plagues, Noah and the Ark, Jonah and the whale, etc. I spent most of this time daydreaming, wishing myself elsewhere. Somehow though, I felt like I knew the Bible. It never occurred to me that you can know Jesus in a personal way or that I really can get help for the confusion and mental anguish I was in. I told myself that I did believe in God, and I would pray from time to time, which basically consisted of me asking God to do something for me. I also thought that by doing what I thought pleased God, He would approve of me, and I would become more spiritual like my mom.

Everyone in my family thought my mom to be the most spiritual person they had ever known. She would make it a point to be constantly praying, fasting, and speaking to the family about their need to come to Christ. In addition to our morning Bible studies, my siblings and I would go with her on Saturday mornings to pass out Gospel Tracts at various locations in the city, while mom preached on her blow horn. I distinctly remember telling people they would go to hell if they didn't have Jesus in their lives, but it never dawned on me to question whether or not I truly knew Jesus. I just did my weekly duty and went on my way, unaware of how much all of these things began to shape the way I would interact with people in the future and view relationships with people—especially with the opposite sex.

Chapter 5

Early Years on My Own

My senior year of high school was a blur. I started cutting classes to wander around the city by myself. I started developing obsessive-compulsive behaviors. I was constantly washing my hands and body. I absolutely hated people touching me in any way, whether that was shaking hands or hugging or just a hand on my shoulder. I wouldn't walk on the cracks of the sidewalk, nor did I come anywhere near grass. I began being attracted to sexual things—an obsession with reading romance novels and all types of risqué magazines and books. It was like a door opened and I fell right in.

After graduating high school and attending a couple of semesters of college, I decided to drop out and joined the U.S. Navy. I had a lot of people in my family that were ex-military and I figured, *Well, if they can do it I most certainly can.* The recruiter was relentless, showing up on my college campus and at my house at all hours of the day. I flew through boot camp and basic training in Great Lakes, Illinois. I had no issues with the physical training as I loved working out, and prior to joining the Navy, I was taking karate lessons with my uncle, an ex-Marine. It gave me a sense of power in a way, and I enjoyed the feeling of pain and pushing the limit of my body. I became a bit of a masochist, I used to think to myself that I would not allow someone to physically hurt me anymore, so working out became an obsession.

After basic training in Great Lakes, I signed up to become a hospital corpsman, which meant I would be staying longer at this location. After completion of corpsman school, I left for Jacksonville, North Carolina to Field Medical Training School. We learned emergency medicine techniques for being out in the field. Our class was scheduled to leave for Iraq because the U.S. military still had troops on the ground over there. I was really excited to go. Besides traveling to Trinidad where my entire family was from, I really hadn't been anywhere else. We found out days before graduation that the class that graduated a week before us would go on to Iraq, but our class would not, which was disappointing. We then had to pick from a list of duty stations where we would be heading after graduation, and by the time it got to me, there wasn't much else left but Newport, Rhode Island. I had never been there, and I figured I would at least be close to home for a while.

I ended up eventually staying there the rest of my enlistment due to the impact Desert Shield had on moving military personnel logistically. During that time, I felt like I had finally thrown off the "nerdy persona" that defined most of my high school experience and became this different person. I started going out with guys and allowing them to touch me even though I barely knew them. It never dawned on me that I was just being used; none of them wanted a relationship with me. In fact, they were all in relationships and just wanted someone they can fool around with.

Toward the end of my eighteen-month tour in Newport, I started dating a young man that I worked with. To protect the innocent, we'll call him "John." John was rough around the edges. He partied hard, smoked weed, and hung out with friends till all hours of the morning drinking and having a good time. Although he was a raw individual, he did have this other side that was sweet and charming. He took his job in the military seriously, but when it was time to party, he was the life of the party, always joking around and pranking our workmates and sometimes random people. I don't remember now how we decided to start dating, but it was over time as we worked together. The relationship was dysfunctional at best, but we kept it going. The atmosphere of the young people in the barracks was that of a never-ending college party. By day, everyone worked in their respective clinics as we were a part of the Naval Clinic on the base, and by evening, the partying began. For some reason, Thursday was the big club night in Rhode Island. People would go off base to the bars right outside the gates, sometimes downtown Newport, some even traveling an hour to Boston or Providence for a good time.

Eventually, the powers that be on the base caught wind of what was going on and the not-so-random urinalysis began. It seemed like the same people would "randomly" be tested every week, sometimes twice a week. This went on for months on the base, until one particular week. It was Super Bowl weekend, an eventful time on the base. Groups of young people would gather together in the barracks or off base at someone's house to watch the game. I really wasn't interested in football at the time, so I never participated in any of these events, and although I knew everyone, I was never really the type to just hang out with large groups of people, but John went. During the evening, the group that he was with began heavily drinking and doing drugs. The next day, we found out that there was going to be another one of those command-wide, not-so-random urinalysis tests. This testing randomly selected all of the young people living in my section of the barracks. John was among that group selected. I can still remember his anxiety as he began to realize what would eventually play out. Over the last couple of months, we saw friends we worked with on-base get busted for drug use and eventually were kicked out of the military. He knew his number was up. Once the urine sample was collected, it took a few days to get the results back. Action on the individual followed very quickly after that.

That afternoon, John and I decided to go to my mom's house, which was about an hour from the base. I'm not sure how it came up in our conversation, but he told my mom he was probably going to get kicked out of the military. I told John that he needed God, and my mom began to quote all of these scriptures from the Bible to him. I could tell he was very nervous. He kept saying that he could not go back to his life back home. A few days later, John ended up meeting a dental tech working at one of the dental clinics on the base. He was a Christian, a real one (not a "whenever it was convenient" churchgoer like myself). John spent a lot of time speaking with this guy at length and told me later on that evening that he had decided to ask Jesus into his heart and wanted to turn his life around. I was pretty skeptical. I mean, honestly John was the last person I ever thought would go to church, and not only just go to church but change. And he did. John radically changed.

He attended church services with the dental tech and his wife, and almost overnight, he began acting and talking differently. He stopped partying and drinking with our friends. The change was so remarkable that it began to trickle through the base. In addition to all of these changes, a few days later, his drug test miraculously came back negative. Some of our friends tested positive but John was negative. He had clearly admitted to his drug usage and was preparing in his mind to go back to Arizona, where he was from. I was floored. How did that happen? If there was anyone that knew about his lifestyle, it was me, and I knew this was a miracle. Now, I'm not saying that you can do drugs, pray, and God will make everything better. But for whatever reason that I have no explanation for, this happened and was witnessed by all of our friends.

John began attending services at a small church about forty-five minutes from the base. He would invite me out to every service three times a week, which at the time seemed like a crazy amount of time to be in church. By this time, I had stopped going to my mom's church. I still considered myself a member, even though I barely went. I just gave up on driving an hour or so to the church every Sunday, especially since I felt like it was not doing me any good. I was so deeply unhappy. I couldn't understand why I felt so empty or why I was constantly battling depression. It was overwhelming at times. I remember John telling me one day in conversation that I always had a dark cloud hanging over my head.

I eventually decided that I would try going to the nondenominational church on base. The church was the complete opposite of my mom's church—quiet and dead as a doornail, but I thought maybe I just need to keep going. I even decided to join the choir at one of my visits, but this barely lasted two months. Soon after I stopped going, I got an invitation to go

Early Years on My Own

to church from one of the ladies I worked with. My coworker was a Jehovah's Witness, and I had grown up debating one of my next-door neighbors on my street whose family was a Jehovah's Witness. They had a large family, and I just couldn't wrap my head around things like not celebrating birthdays or only 144,000 people going into heaven or the heaven-on-earth theory. It just didn't make sense to me. Needless to say, I declined her invitation, and we started arguing doctrine a lot. I wasn't a Bible scholar by any stretch of the imagination, but I always managed to find some Scripture to make my argument work.

Through all of this, John kept going to church with the dental tech and his wife. Six months passed, and he continued to invite me to go with him. Even though I saw how drastically he changed, I wouldn't go. As the months passed, typical to any new Christian, your old life begins to pull at you again. John had returned to the base from a trip home to Arizona. He had dyed his dirty blond hair red and told all of us that he was no longer going to attend the church he had been going to off base. For some unknown reason, this really bothered me. He began to say that he wasn't so sure any more about some of the things he had started to believe in, and invited me to come to check out a different church. I began to question him. What in the world was going on? John told me that he had met up with one of his best friends on his trip, who also started going to church, and that church had a branch in Rhode Island. John explained that they had talked in-depth, and he thought this church might be better for him. Sunday came, and John, a girl we worked with, and I decided to check out John's new church.

People were hugging each other and singing for much of the service. I don't remember much of the sermon as it was more of a talk. Everyone seemed fake, like they were trying really hard to be a Christian. After the sermon, they invited anyone who wanted to have a new life in Christ to come forward to be baptized in a large trough at the front of the church. I would learn later that the church believed salvation came by way of baptism. I told John later that I wasn't so sure about the church—I couldn't handle the lovey-dovey way people were acting, and I just couldn't believe you have to be baptized to be forgiven of your sins (and I still don't). The only thing I really remember from my old church and listening to the TV preachers growing up was a verse in Romans: "'that if you confess with your mouth the Lord Jesus and believe in your heart that God has raised Him from the dead, you will be saved. For with the heart one believes unto righteousness, and with the mouth confession is made unto salvation.'" (Romans 10:9-10, NKJV). This became a subject of deep discussion between us. What if there wasn't a means to baptism? Does this mean there is no pathway to God? After a couple of weeks, John stopped going. About a week later, John had a visitor on base. It was the pastor from the church John was originally going to. I was so surprised to see him standing outside of the barracks. He introduced himself and said that he was going to visit John. I said something along the lines of, "Yeah, he really needs some help." In my mind, John was all gone. I remember thinking to myself, *I don't think I ever really had a conversation with the pastor of the church I used to go to, and I never had anyone in the church reach out to me, ever.* I asked John about the visit later, and he told me that the pastor just wanted to check on him. I never knew pastors did that. I found it hard to believe that a pastor genuinely cared about people in that manner. *What a stark contrast from my mom, the now newly minted reverend, preaching hell fire on the streets.* This made me curious to find out more about the church.

Chapter 6

Salvation

Although I decided to check the church out, it would be a few months before I actually did. First, I attended a concert that they were putting on at a park in the area. It was really the first time I spent time with "church" people outside of a church setting. There was someone playing the guitar and singing songs that were familiar, but with lyrics that spoke to the love of Christ and the need for Him. Others folks were walking around speaking to people in the park about Jesus and inviting them out to the services but not in the same manner of my experience with my mom. I heard words like "God wants a relationship with you." "It's possible to experience change." They took the time to converse and interact with people. A couple of weeks later, I accepted an invite from John to go to the pastor's house. A group of people from the church was going to spend some time just hanging out and playing some board games with their family. This really made me curious. For some reason, I didn't think pastors had fun or spent time with people like that in a casually manner. Everyone at the house was really nice and welcoming. The pastor at one point in the evening offered me hot dogs. Now at this point in my life, the obsessive-compulsive tendencies I started developing toward the end of high school was now in full force. I didn't even consider how rude I was being, I was controlled by my mind and I couldn't bring myself to eat it simply because he had touched it. The plate sat there, untouched, the entire evening.

A few weeks later, I went to a Sunday morning service. It was so different, I felt like I couldn't wrap my mind around it. I was used to services that lasted four to five hours. People would be "overcome" with the spirit so much so that they couldn't control their actions or body and would be dropping like flies on the floor all around you. Inevitably, someone would start dancing in the aisles, others would be waving flags or handkerchiefs, jumping, spinning, or even crying uncontrollably. A lot of this stuff happened while the pastor was preaching.

At this church, there wasn't any of that. There was a time of singing and praising God, but no emotional outbursts or overboard hugging or anything like that. People actually sat and listened to the preaching. I didn't know what to think! I concluded maybe they were out of touch with how church was supposed to be. Everyone was really nice and encouraging, but also real. They didn't shy away from the fact that they had issues and things they were dealing with, knowing there was hope in Christ to change these circumstances. I really appreciated that because I often felt like church people always acted like they didn't have real life issues. I went out to a few more Sunday morning services. I still didn't know what to make of all of this in terms of what I was going to do with it, but the one thing I did know was that I was just miserable. I could no longer control my obsessive-compulsive behaviors, and I felt like it was just choking me. Besides constantly washing my hands from all sorts of germs, real or imagined, I started obsessively cleaning. I would be up at all hours of the night cleaning my space in the barracks over and over again. I took stock in Lysol products. I didn't like anyone touching anything that was mine. It was an internal prison.

After service one morning, the pastor asked to borrow a pen from me to write some information down. When he gave it back, I immediately pulled out antibacterial wipes that I always carried in my purse to wipe the pen down. Along with these obsessions came an ever-present sense of fear, I was fearful of dying and fearful of touching people, which that in itself was strange because I had a boyfriend. But there were times I didn't even want him to hold my hand. I always felt ashamed and condemned because I knew the things we were doing in our relationship weren't morally right.

I was constantly praying for forgiveness, but I was never free. I became fixated on certain thoughts, some very sexual in nature, others very dark and disturbing that I couldn't clear my mind. I would constantly replay things in my head that happened to me. I had heard one time from a TV preacher that there were certain sins that, once committed, were unforgiveable, and I felt there was no chance God can forgive me for all the things I had done. This constantly played in my mind. I couldn't control any of my thoughts. I feared that I would end up in a mental institution like some members of my family. Out of my mom's eight other siblings, two of them had completely lost their minds. They broke mentally because of things that occurred in their lives and lived full time in mental institutions.

One of them had a child who had lived with us in the big house my grandparents owned. She was a year older than me and went to live with her father when her mom had a nervous breakdown. I met up with her in high school and she ended up having a nervous breakdown herself, missing a lot of her high school years. I thought of her often and felt at times I would eventually end up going down the same road. There seemed to be no way out and this led to depression—hopelessness so deep there were times I didn't even want to get out of bed and go about the day. But being in the military, I had no choice. Nothing anyone said to me seemed able to change the situation. As I contemplated my life, I began to have suicidal thoughts. There didn't seem to be a point of living. I had no value or self-worth, and I was unable to stay a Christian. I went so far as to plan out how I would take my life, and the night I was going to go through with it, my mom called, right before I did it. As I knew her to be the most spiritual person in my family, I thought this must be a sign from God. How else would she know what I was going to do?

I hadn't gone to John's church in a while, but one afternoon while we were working, John invited one of our coworkers and me to a Sunday night service. He told me that there would be a pastor preaching at the church that was leaving to become a missionary in Africa with his family. This was so intriguing to me. I had never met a missionary and wondered what it took to do this. My friend and I decided to go to the service. As I sat in the service and listened to the preacher, I thought to myself: *he really believes what he is saying.* He is literally going to give up his life to go to Africa with his wife and young daughter. They seemed so excited about this. His wife was really pretty and so genuinely nice. His desire for God was almost tangible; it just really touched me. Toward the end of the service, he gave a call to anyone

Salvation

that didn't know Christ to accept this invitation to ask Him into their heart.

I had prayed a prayer to ask Jesus into my heart so many times and in so many places including with televangelists. But this time around this was different. I wanted to know God the way that preacher knew God. I was desperate for help and for the first time in my life I actually believed that God would help me. So, I prayed that night—August 9, 1998—and I asked Jesus into my heart to forgive me and to change me. I went back to the base, and the guest preacher, his wife, and their little girl headed off to Africa that week.

That week, I began to pray every day. I can't say I felt the heavens open up. On the contrary, I began to feel a bit of confusion. What should I do now? I went back the next Sunday and afterwards, I decided I would call my mom. I began to tell her about the church and my decision to ask Jesus into my heart. She really didn't understand what I was saying as I really couldn't explain fully why I did this. My mom expressed that we grew up hearing about God and going to church, so "what exactly was my issue?" As the months went on, I kept going to the church. At first, I just went to my usual Sunday morning, then eventually both services on Sunday. Before long, I was going to the mid-week services on Thursday evenings in addition to Sundays. I didn't mind the hour drive or the tolls we paid along the way; I knew I needed this. I remember talking briefly to the pastor after church service. I was always a bit afraid of him as I didn't feel yet that I could trust him. I remember rallying myself to ask him questions about the church and what was going on with me mentality. He told me to keep coming and to read my Bible.

And what exactly is that going to do? I asked myself. After all, in my mind, I had read the Bible my whole life. The reality was I really hadn't read the Bible as much as I told myself I did. My supposed expertise came from the little I remembered from the Bible stories my mom would read to us and whatever I caught on television or hearsay. In fact, I found Bible reading to be kind of tedious and boring. But I gave it a try. Romans was the first book I began reading, and it was shocking. The words seemed to come alive. For the first time in my life, I actually realized that I understood fully what I was reading and the implications. I couldn't stop reading. *Where was this my whole life? Why didn't I know this, and do people know what it says in here?* The revelation was profound, and it made me question what I grew up believing. Every day, I would open the Bible and read. The more I read, the more I began to realize how far I had been from God and how much I did not know who He was.

I began to have what I can only describe as a hunger to know God. I would call my mom after every service and tell her what the pastor had preached about and what I read in the Bible. I respected her opinion as she had become a reverend in her church, but as I continued going to church, my mom's attitude toward the church began to change from understanding and encouragement to concern that I was in a cult. I had begun to question some of the teachings she believed as I compared them to what I was reading in the Bible and they weren't adding up. The more I questioned her, the more she began to tell me she didn't think I was in the right church. I felt surprised by this as I expected her to be happy that I was no longer miserable and depressed.

One weekend, mom asked me to come home and speak to my old pastor. The pastor always scared me as she had a way about her that was very intimidating and unapproachable. As the three of us sat down and started speaking, she pulled out this massive Bible and began to ask me all these questions about the church I had started going to. Soon her

Salvation

and I began going back and forth about all kinds of doctrinal issues. She finally ended the discussion, as my mom sat and watched us, by telling me she saw a vision of me surrounded by all of these people that I think are my friends at the church, but they are not my friends and they will end up hurting me. I knew right then and there that I made the right decision in leaving my old church. I thought back to the nonexistent relationships, people that I had tried hard to befriend who never spoke to me and treated me like they were better. I told her people do hurt each other in life but at least I was going somewhere where I didn't feel invisible and people actually went out of their way to ask me how I was doing. At least they weren't fake. My mom and I didn't speak for a few months after this as I needed time to process of all this, and she believed me to be brainwashed as she often said.

As I continued going to the church, I began to tell others on the base about my new life in Christ. I just had this desire to tell others. One of the turning points in my life during this time, besides asking Jesus to be my Savior, was the day I decided to get baptized. I realized baptism was not salvation, which is the repentance of sin and accepting what Jesus did on the cross, but symbolic of the shedding of my old life and turning toward the new one in Christ. I had gotten baptized in my mom's church, and honestly, I don't remember much of the day other than being embarrassed that my hair become an instant afro once I went into the water, and my skin turning ash white from the water hitting severely dry skin.

As I headed to the pond with others from the church, I didn't even mind that I was walking on the cracks of the sidewalk at first. When we got to the edge of the pond, it was more rocky than sandy. There was seaweed everywhere, typical of New England coastal waters. As I gazed at all the seaweed and rocks, I could feel myself starting to freak out inside. I realized that I had to walk out into the water barefoot. I wanted to die—I hated walking barefoot. If I thought that grass was bad, all of this seaweed and rocks were like another level in my mind. I realized that I had to make a decision. God was real, and He would help me. When it was my turn, I went into the water. I turned and faced the people at the water's edge. As I came up out of the water, I felt this sense of freedom. I can only describe it as a weight being lifted from me, something I had never felt before. I walked forward and picked up a massive pile of seaweed that was floating around me and just dumped it over my head. For the first time in my life, I realized that I could be free. I didn't have to live with all of these obsessive-compulsive behaviors that ruled my life. I got out of the water and walked over to a patch of grass near the pond and stuck my feet in. It actually felt good.

As I continued going to church, slowly things in my life began to change. I could not get enough of God, church, and everything happening at church. Thursdays and Sundays were off-limits for work, and I lost my second job I was working while in the military because of it. I wanted to go to church. On base, John and I would tell everyone and anyone about Jesus. More people started going to the church with us from the base. We started carpooling to church with another couple we'd told about Jesus. They were on the brink of divorce and as they had started going to church with us, they began to see that Jesus could move and help the brokenness of their marriage. The four of us were known as the "Gospel Gangsters" on base. The church began really growing as we would bring anyone who would listen to the church. We were really excited about growing in our relationship with Christ and the impact we were having on the base.

Chapter 7

Call For My Life

About six months after I started going to church, I found out that there would be a weeklong Bible conference at one of our churches in Cape Cod, Massachusetts. Never having gone to anything like that, I was pretty curious. A lot of people at church were going to go, so I requested the time off and went as well. I stayed the week at the home of a single mom and her three daughters. I didn't know what to expect, but she was so nice. She really made me feel at ease. She was so excited about the conference, and we spent a lot of time that week talking about all sorts of things. She attended the church faithfully with her daughters, who were all in their teens and involved in all that was happening at the church. I could tell that they looked forward to going, and it was very much a part of their lives in terms of how they lived. The teens were not boy-crazy and detached but very excited about the conference. I was so used to the family dysfunction I grew up with that I almost thought something was wrong with them.

The conference really blew me away. There were so many people there from all over the East Coast and even overseas. All gathered together to hear four sermons a day for five straight days. There was excitement in the air as people reconnected with old friends and made new ones. I really felt like our church back home was a part of something much bigger than us. It was a lot to process, but in the same breath, I wanted to be a part of it all. During the time I was going to my new church, I never really spoke in depth to the pastor and his wife, but being at the conference all week, I began to find out more about them and where our church fit in the bigger picture of the conference. Pastor Frank Luna and his wife Belen had moved to Rhode Island to start a church from El Paso, Texas. They had no family in New England and really didn't know where Rhode Island was prior to coming. I had never met anyone who had done something like that. Why would they move all the way here, sight unseen, to open a church?

They shared that they felt God called them here. This was new to me. *God actually cared what you did with your life?* It sounded like a Moses or Abraham kind of thing. It didn't stop at the conference. There were many couples like them that were pastoring at other churches throughout New England and up and down the East Coast. I was even more blown away by one of the guest speakers at the conference, Pastor Wyman Mitchell. I had never heard anyone preach like him. He had such a knowledge of God's Word and was unpretentious, which very much appealed to me. Pastor Mitchell had a way of preaching that made you think. He always referenced the Bible.

I inquired about him and found out that Pastor Mitchell was sent to pastor a small church that was falling apart in the middle of nowhere in Prescott, Arizona in the seventies. He began seeking God for the church and his ministry and began to reach out to the young people that were just lost but searching for answers during that time. This coincided with what was called the "Jesus People Movement," where thousands of youths were turning from the social issues and drug culture of the hippie days to seeking truth and conservative forms of Christianity. The church in Prescott began to grow as young people there started turning to Jesus and were filled with excitement to share Jesus with the world. Pastor Mitchell began sending couples out of Prescott to start churches in various cities and these churches, in turn, began spreading the hope of change through Jesus, sending couples out of their churches to do the same. This blossomed into a massive fellowship of churches around the globe whose purpose was to spread the gospel of Christ.

This was nothing I had ever seen before, and I wanted to be a part of it. For the first time in my life, I began to grasp that Jesus wasn't just for myself and the four walls of our church, but for everyone. For years, I considered myself a Christian based on the fact that I believed in God, but I had never experienced conversion or a change. I had never experienced a change in my heart, life, and way of thinking that impacted who I was as a person. Toward the end of the week, I began praying and asking God to show me if He had something for my life. I thought back to the couple who came through my home church en route to Africa and I really wanted that for my life. I prayed every opportunity I had for myself, and I really felt like God had put that in my heart. On the last day of the conference, I went to Pastor Luna's wife, Belen, and I told her that I felt called to be a missionary.

She was super encouraging and told me that was great! And I felt such a joy unlike anything I had really experienced in my life. I felt like I had a purpose in my life now. We were all excited and encouraged by our experiences and to see what we were a part of. A lot of my friends expressed a desire to go out and pastor a church like the couples we had all met during the week. One of the other realizations I had come to that week was the need to figure out where John and I were headed in our relationship. By this point, we had been dating for two years. We decided to talk to Pastor Luna about our relationship and did so the very next service at our church. Pastor asked us if we were thinking of moving forward in our relationship, perhaps getting married. I remember thinking to myself, *Well of course we are going to get married. I loved John, and I wanted to be a missionary. This shouldn't be an issue.* John and I agreed to get together to talk about the next steps. As the weeks passed my optimism about marriage soon became bleak. John was avoiding talking about the situation until I finally said we needed to talk.

He then told me that not only was he not ready for marriage, but he also wasn't even certain I was the one for him. He did not love me in that way. I was crushed—didn't expect this, as I thought John and I were on the same page. We agreed to break up. At first I felt hurt, but pretty soon, those emotions turned to anger and then bitterness toward him. It wasn't long before he became interested in other girls at church. *What the heck did they have that I didn't?* I would constantly ask myself. It was really hard to control the anger at times as we were always together in some form. We lived in the same barracks, I saw him at every church service, and we became involved in Bible studies and outreaches into the community; there was no getting away from him. All I could think of was after all that time and everything we had been through, *Are you kidding me?* The anger was so strong that I would try and get other people not to talk to John at church or on base. As the months passed, I realized that I was still having a hard time letting go of John and I needed help. I decided to call Pastor Luna. My issue was much deeper than breaking up with John. That situation resurrected the deep-rooted issues from my childhood that I thought were all cleared up. At the center was rejection. I had felt rejected by John, but also in my past, that constant desire to fit in, be noticed, and have attention. I was able to talk it through with pastor and his wife, and they prayed for me to let go of the anger and past hurts, allowing God to heal my heart. I laid my heart on the altar that evening, and as I left their house, I never felt another emotion toward John other than friendship. In fact, as time passed, he eventually got married and I ended up in a music group at church with him and his wife.

John and I ended our relationship in April of 1999. A few months later, I decided not to reenlist in the military. My extension was up, I had a year left of active duty service, and any duty station or ship I would have chosen would require me to extend my enlistment for another year or two. Although I really wanted to get stationed in Japan, I decided it was probably best that I get out. With this mind, I submitted a request to finish out my last year in Rhode Island and to get out of the military after that. What scared me about getting out was the fact that I didn't have a college degree or any specific skills other than those learned in the military. A pathway for a job seemed unrealistic. I wanted to go back to college, but this required me to move back home after I got out, and this wasn't something I wanted to do. I was already very independent.

The area of Boston I grew up in was very tough. I did not want to go back to that life, I knew I would get caught up again. I asked Pastor Luna for direction, and he advised me to pray about it and told me that if it was God's will that I stay, He will open doors for me and make it possible. I felt a bit frustrated as I honestly just wanted him to tell me what choice I should make. Prior to becoming a Christian, I never included God in my day-to-day living. Before I made major life decisions, I never once stopped and considered if this was something God wanted me to do. I just lived and did what I thought was best. But as I began growing in my relationship with God, I began to realize that in order for God to be the central focus of life, He needed to be in my decisions and plans. For all of those years I spent in church growing up, I was aware of right and wrong, but I never wondered if something I was doing was what God pictured. So, I prayed. One of the things that I learned early on in my walk with Christ was that living for Him requires faith. In Hebrews 11:1 (ESV), the author writes, "Now faith is the substance of things hoped for, the evidence of things not seen." And also, in verse 6, "But without faith, it is impossible to please him, for whoever would draw near to God must believe that he exists and that he rewards those who seek him."

    As I prayed, I didn't feel anything. Again, the heavens did not open up and tell me what to do. I didn't have a sign drop down in front of me. I just thought about my situation, and I remember thinking *Well, if God wanted me to do this, then He would have to open a door*, so I submitted the paperwork to confirm the end of my enlistment, and I told my family I would be staying in Rhode Island. About a week later, John—who got out of the military himself a few months before me—came up to me and offered to speak with our former supervisor from one of the clinics we used to work in, on the base about a job for me, and that's exactly what happened. I got hired at an eye clinic in Providence about a week before I was due to get out, and I also managed to secure an apartment near the church not far from work that same week. God had worked it out, and I was right back working with John again at an eye clinic, bringing back memories of when we first met. The way things work out in life can be really funny sometimes. I was encouraged to see God come through for me in making a difficult decision. I felt hope for the future.

Chapter 8

Moving On

As a civilian, I was able to be fully committed to all we were doing at church. I still wanted to go back to college, but I knew I would not be able to work full time, go to college, *and* keep my commitments at church as the church was starting to grow. I wanted to participate in the weekly concert and drama scene at church, help with those new to the faith, and be a part of outreach in the local community. I decided that I would focus on my job and maybe somewhere down the line, I would go back to college. A lot of my family did not understand my decision. They thought it was crazy to stay at a small church with a guy I had broken up with who didn't want to marry me and watch him be interested in other women. They couldn't understand why I would not move back to Massachusetts where I could have gone back to school for free at the time, instead of staying in a place

Moving On

with no relatives and a menial job (in their opinion). One day while I was at work, I received a call from one of my aunts and her husband. They called to check on me and as we started speaking, my aunt cut in and began to say, "Kizzy, in case no one ever told you, I will: You have made the biggest mistake with your life. A complete failure."

When I hung up the phone, I was so hurt, no matter how I tried to explain my decisions, it fell on deaf ears. I had to just give it to God. I knew I had experienced a change in my life, and I was not willing to give that up.

Two years after John and I broke up, I began dating a guy at my church. I'll call him "Andrew" to protect the innocent. By now, I no longer worked with John at the eye clinic in Providence. I began a career as an insurance agent. I knew Andrew pretty well as he was friends with John. He was one of the groups of people we started bringing to church from the base, and he was committed to serving God as well. We had a great friendship, and I was actually pretty surprised when he expressed interest in me. We went out on a couple of dates. He was always a gentleman, opening doors, very polite, and was a good listener. We talked a lot about our relationship with God, the church, and what we thought our lives would hold. I told him of my dream to be a missionary in Africa, and he said that he felt like God was calling him to do the same. About a month after we started dating, he found out that he was to leave to go to Iraq and left a few weeks later for training in Jacksonville, North Carolina.

About a month later, he had a deployment date, and I drove down to North Carolina with a few people to see him off. We would talk on a daily basis by phone, email, and by letters when he was deployed. Upon his return to the U.S., which was only a couple of months later, he went back to the base in North Carolina. I was so excited he was back and safe.

He was attending one of our churches in North Carolina, and we began conversing by phone again. A couple of weeks after he had gotten back, he stopped calling and emailing me. I would call and there would be no response. I would send out emails to no response, nothing. By December 2002, it was over. At the church conference in the Cape a few months later, I met someone from the church in North Carolina who knew Andrew, and she told me that he was interested in another girl. He was with her all the time, and they had started dating a few months back. It turns out she was also writing to him during his deployment.

I was hurt and angry, but there was a difference this time around. I had never crossed any lines morally with Andrew, so although I was upset and hurt, I was able to move on quickly. I told God one evening I was done with dating, that I don't want to date another guy unless He tells me he is my husband. I don't know if it's biblical or not, but I didn't want to date unless I know. And so the wait began. Andrew came back to Rhode Island to visit some friends and the church a few years later. He had married the other woman and she was pregnant with their first child. He never said anything to me. It was like I never existed. Rejection can really hurt, but I have learned it is important how you process what happens. I had a choice to make. I could dwell on these past relationships and not let go, or I could give it to God.

As hard as it was not to dwell on being rejected, I knew I had to move forward. As I made friends with other single ladies in some of our neighboring churches, I realized we all dealt with various issues, but at the heart of it, most people have a desire for a relationship and a family. We would all talk about what we would do when we got married and what we envisioned our wedding day to be like—the excitement of doing God's will, seeing God's plan unfold for our lives as a couple.

    I very much still hung on to my dream of being a missionary, and I thought to myself, *Well it will just be a matter of time.* Our church was near the airport and almost every time I would drive past the airport, I would dream of myself leaving to pastor a church with my husband and family abroad. It was during this time, I met a young woman at the church in the Cape who had just started dating a guy from one of our churches in Connecticut. She was so excited to be dating this guy, and shortly after, they were married. They had started coming to our church temporarily before transitioning back to the Cape. One afternoon she showed me her wedding album and told me "It was so worth the wait!" She was twenty-nine and had waited a long time to get married. I can remember thinking to myself, *Wow! That's a long time to wait. I wonder if that will happen to me.* She also told me that she had prayed to marry a Marine since she was a teenager, and God gave her a Marine. I thought about that for a long time. I never considered actually praying for specific attributes or qualities in someone. Nevertheless, I wrote a list of what I wanted in my husband, and I believed that God would give me exactly what I prayed for. I thought about my friend getting married at almost thirty. That was six years away for me. Could I really wait that long?

Chapter 9

Turning Thirty

In 2007, I turned thirty. I was excited to leave my twenties behind and embark on my journey forward in life. I had stability in my life as I was working a good job, our church was growing. I was excited about the future. I thought often about getting married and figured, *Well, it will be a matter of time before I meet someone.* I mean, after all, I was entering my thirties. I had plenty of time. I tried to finish my college education. Although I didn't actually need this it for my job, it was just one of those things I wanted for myself. I had put it on hold to stay in Rhode Island and just focus on my newfound relationship with God and involvement in the church. I knew a lot of people worked and went to school, but I knew I wasn't really focused at that time in order to do that. I remember giving this desire to God and just saying, "You know I really want to pursue this, but I'm unable to . . . If there is a way in the future, then I'll continue," and that was very difficult to do because I really wanted to continue my education. So, at the age of thirty, I signed up to pursue a computer science degree program. Getting the enrollment confirmation from the school was so exciting.

> Tue, Nov 27, 2007 10:02 am
> kizzy moraldo xxxxxxx@gmail.com
> To B. Luna xxxxxx@hotmail.com, Ileana xxxxx@ridsi.necoxmail. com
>
> I have also now officially become a cry baby . . . . today I read the "Your Enrolled!" email and I had to go in the bathroom and cry . . . well actually because I was so overwhelmed and thankful that after all these years(graduated from high school 13 years ago) God has just opened a door for me to do something that has just been a little dream tucked away in my heart for a long time, not that I plan to go conquer the world with an education, it really is just something I wanted to do just for me. so even now as I write I'm in tears . . . I think it's just a little ironic that I'm busier now than I have ever been in my life and also older than I ever thought I would be so I'm hoping that I'll do well, and not forget everything else in my life. I also got confirmation from the VA that they received my application for education benefits and it's in Processing, so hopefully, that will happen quickly!! (timeframe is 10-12 weeks) so I just wanted to share . . . If anyone wants to cry with me, I'll be available after work. Thanks for listening.
> Kizzy
> Student ID ###548

I was able to go using my education benefits through the military and kept my full-time job. I was still committed to my involvement with the church. It was important to me to see the church grow. We were involved in a lot of local and out-of-town outreaches with some of our area churches. The church's footprint had expanded in Rhode Island; as four more churches were added, for a total of five, and even more in Massachusetts. Most of the couples were among my peers. Some of them grew up in the church while others had come in and given their lives to Christ in their late teens or very early twenties, married only a short time but committed to advancing the gospel.

It was so exciting, and I was so happy to be a part of helping them outreach for special services. Adding school to this was very difficult, but I felt like I was more mature, had a lot of drive, and a whole lot more discipline than in my twenties. It was exhausting at times, but being single, I was able to juggle all of it. By the time I was thirty-two, it had been years since the Andrew break-up, and pretty much all of my friends except my roommate had gotten married. I remember going to one of my best friend's wedding where I was one of the bridesmaids and thinking *Wow, she is like one of the last ones besides myself and my roommate in my group of peers at church to get married.* I was so happy for her because, like me, she had waited into her late twenties, and we would often talk about marriage and doing God's will. And it was encouraging to see that fulfilled in her life . . . I just knew my time was coming, but had not yet arrived.

One afternoon, I went over to Pastor Luna and Belen's home to babysit. After twenty-one years of marriage and wanting a baby, Pastor Luna and Belen finally had a little girl. She was an absolute joy to their lives, her coming into their lives was an absolute miracle. I was so amazed at how they were able to wait so long. I asked Belen one day, how was she able to wait so long. But not just waiting, but believing God to bless them with a child for so long as they had been told many times, through other pastors and in their prayer lives, that they would have a child. She told me she realized she had to be content in God. That fulfillment came through Christ and not just through having something even though she wanted it. That was amazing to me because I could honestly say I felt like I wavered between discontentment and contentment, especially when I thought about what I wanted in life.

As I arrived. They were going to dinner with the pastor from the church in Cape Cod as he was flying out to a church conference. The church in the Cape was always a reference point for our church. I had a lot of friends in the church and they were always helping the smaller area churches as it was a very large church. Lots of talent was found in that church from professional musicians, business owners, teachers, artists, and the like. I really saw that Jesus was for everyone at that church, no matter where you were in life. In greeting the pastor of the Cape Church, I remember him grasping my hand and telling me that God sees me. He sees that I have watched everyone around me getting married and going forward, and that in my life, God saved the best for last. I literally burst into tears because just before I had pulled up to Pastor Luna's house, I was specifically thinking of all of my friends that had gotten married the last few years and our changing relationships as we weren't just single girls hanging out anymore. Everything had become finding out what their spouse was doing, or they were doing things with other married couples instead. I know that's the healthy way marriage works, but as someone still in the "single" scene, I missed the care-free days. I felt like God met me right where I was, and it was pretty incredible because I hadn't spoken to anyone about what I was thinking or feeling. I went home that evening and wrote that down in my journal. I would later understand what that meant as I pondered the pastor's words through the years.

Chapter 10

Passing of Time

Turning thirty-five was another turning point for me. As my birthday approached, I began to think about what I was doing with my life and where it was headed. I had been a Christian now for fourteen years. The years seemed to have blinked by, and suddenly I was in my mid-thirties. Even though life was busy, at the same time, I felt like it was also on pause. I had a prayer life, I was faithful to church, involved with everything going on, but inside I felt like I was in such a dry place, a desert. I started wondering what happened to my dream of being a missionary. What happened to me getting married? Why was I still single after all this time? Did God not see my desires? In all of my busyness, did I somehow miss the boat? Maybe I haven't prayed enough about this. '

Along with these thoughts, I also began to think about church. The church seemed to be a strange place. Over the last year, for some reason or another, a lot of people had just stopped coming. For a time, it seemed like we had more people leaving than coming and staying. One of the couples that left was John and his wife. John said he felt God was moving him and his wife, who was pregnant at the time, to North Carolina. I felt such sadness as he was the last of the people left in the church that had gotten saved with me from the Navy base all those years ago. And as sure as he felt it was God calling him to leave, I felt in my heart it wasn't. John became upset when I voiced that something about his leaving didn't feel right not because of any attachment to me—those feelings were long gone—but because there was more to the story, and I would come to find out later there was.

In the year or so after they left, there continued to be a real struggle in our church. It seemed so difficult to see people come in, give their lives to Christ, come back a few more times, then disappear. This seemed to trickle down to some of our other churches in the area as they began to close. Couples that were my friends, who had gotten married and sent out into the ministry way back, were now back in their home church or starting a church somewhere else. Within a few years, all of the churches closed in Rhode Island with the exception of ours. It seemed like we went from five churches to one almost overnight.

What was God's plan in all of this? It seemed like the more I prayed, the thicker the wall felt between God and my prayers. For one of the rare moments in my life, I considered leaving Rhode Island. Perhaps I just was not in the right place anymore. Perhaps as life was evolving, I needed to do the same. As I struggled with what I should do, I realized I just needed to do what I know to do. As human beings, when we feel like things are not happening, we want to do something to change the situation ourselves. And in some circumstances, that is appropriate, but I have learned that when it comes to making big decisions, the time to do this is not when you are emotional, not in the middle of a major crisis or turmoil. Instead, in these moments, we are called to bring our situations, frustrations, questions, and our life to God. And this can be the greatest area of struggle as trusting God despite what we see is easier said than done. But God calls us to trust.

"Trust in the Lord with all your heart and lean not on your own understanding; In all your ways acknowledge Him, And He shall direct your paths" (Proverbs 3:5-6, NKJV). Trust is having a firm belief in the truth, reliability, and strength of someone as defined by Oxford Language dictionaries. It's easy to trust in the Lord when life's going great and things are working out as desired but that isn't true trust. Anyone can do that. True trust in God is displayed when things are not working out as planned or the complete opposite is happening. As I pondered these things, I thought about the second area of struggle in my life and that was the silence. Silence can be deafening in that you began to imagine what's not there. I struggled with this as I perceived God as not hearing my prayers. Nothing was happening that I felt should be happening. Why were all these people leaving the church? There wasn't some new doctrine being introduced. The church was a vital part of my existence and a big part of the reason for my staying in Rhode Island, but if things weren't working out the way I think they should, does that mean I should leave as well? What about the fact that I have been praying about all of this and I have not gotten an answer to my prayers? So, does no answer mean a "yes" to what I think I should do?

Passing of Time

Having an analytic mind can be a blessing and a curse. I have not done things often in life because I sat and analyzed every aspect of the situation to the point it passes me by. Other times it has saved me from making major mistakes. In all of this, I came to a place where I realized if I have issues with trust and I am perceiving silence, maybe I need to just wait on God and ask Him to help me with these issues. In the book of Isaiah, it says, "But those who wait on the Lord shall renew their strength; They shall mount up with wings like eagles, they shall run and not be weary, They shall walk and not faint" (Isaiah 40:31, NKJV).

I know that God answers prayers. This has been evident in my life over the years and in the lives of others. But God's answer isn't always "Yes." Sometimes it's "No," and other times it is simply "Not now." Silence does not mean that God does not see or is not in control. Silence does not mean punishment as we are in difficult places and God's not just zapping us out of it. Often our concept of God is within the scope of our limited understanding as humans. We think we have God all figured out, but in reality, we have not even tapped into the vastness of who He is. It seems illogical to do nothing but wait on God. And this doesn't mean that you do not live, or you just pull back. Continue to seek God for His plan as you live, pray, read God's Word, and share Jesus with the lost. I was guilty of not doing things in my life because I was waiting to get married to do those things with a special someone. I remember someone asking me one day, "Well, what if he doesn't come?" There are people who do not get married. In the end, my anxiety and concerns over what was going on with church and the perceived impenetrable silence in my life had to be left with God.

Around this time, I had started a new job. After working as an insurance agent for many years, servicing personal insurance policies dealing with homeowners, cars, boats, motorcycles, and small business insurance clients. I was ready for a change and came across an opening to work with large commercial accounts and healthcare systems. It was difficult at first working in a corporate company. But within a year and a half of starting the new job, my salary increased by almost ten percent, and another five percent the following year. My salary increases opened the door for me to purchase a home. This was a big decision for me as I never thought I would have the income to be able to do this alone, and I had always imagined it as part of life's progression after marriage. As life would eventually play out, the decision to purchase a home would affect more than just me.

In addition to working through a new job, starting the process of homebuying, fighting through school, and being involved in the church, I began dealing with severe iron deficiency, causing extreme fatigue. I had struggled on and off with anemia due to heavy menstrual cycles over the years, but now it was like I turned a corner, and everything was at another level. I made an appointment with my primary care doctor and gynecologist. I went through the process of blood work, exams, ultrasounds, and the results were that I had developed a few small fibroids. The gynecologist told me that the fibroids were so small, they shouldn't cause the level of blood loss that I was experiencing. He suggested trying birth control pills to control the heaviness of the cycle. The side effects were immediate.

I became more fatigued, foggy, and started experiencing joint pain throughout my body. Within a few months, I was experiencing so much blood loss that I was taking upwards of three pills a day to try and stop the bleeding. We switched the type of birth control a few times in the months that followed to try to find something that would work. This went on for months. One of the last things I decided to try was an intrauterine device (IUD), which stopped the cycle, but the effects continued. I reached a point where I would sleep in my car during my lunch breaks at work. I could barely keep my eyes open to study and complete assignments for school. After almost two years of living in a fog, I decided one morning that I was done. I made an appointment with my gynecologist to remove the IUD. What should have been an in-office visit ended up being a surgical procedure, as it was stuck and couldn't be removed in the office.

As I was still losing a significant amount of blood each month, I began a series of iron infusions to help with the anemia. After having a severe reaction to the infusion during the first round, I was able to find a hospital in Boston where they were able to pre-medicate me before receiving the infusions twice a week. This continued every few months until I decided to have the small fibroids removed. Although my doctor kept explaining they were so small they couldn't be causing my issues, I wasn't convinced, and decided to get a second opinion. I could no longer live with the fog. To this day I still have no idea how I was able to hold down a job, make it church, and continue with my course work at school. After receiving a second opinion I decided to have the fibroids removed. Turns out I actually had thirteen fibroids, with the majority of them inside the uterus, not really visible in the ultrasound and scans I had done. I remember the surgeon telling me that the goal was to save the uterus as I was thirty-five and may still want children. She told me that my window to get pregnant was very short as the older I got, the more difficult it would be. When she asked if I wanted children, I told her I did, and that I was a Christian who really believed God could bring that person into my life. I just knew that the right person would come along. I didn't know how she would react, but she turned to me and said "You know what? So am I."

Recovering from the surgery was a breeze for me. I had been in so much pain for so long, it literally felt like nothing, and before long, I felt like I was back on track. I began to pray in earnest for a husband. I felt like the clock was ticking and my chances to start a family were shrinking. Surely God sees what I am dealing with.

Later on that year, I decided to go to the annual church conference at the church on the Cape. I was determined to meet someone. I hadn't gone in several years as I was dealing with being so sick. Sitting in the service the first night, I began to feel strange. I felt like time had passed as I was standing still. Of course, I knew that life moves forward, but it's so strange how in our brains, we picture people exactly the way we last saw them. Being sick for so long and not seeing a lot of folks over several years, I realized that the kids who were five, six, or seven when I had gotten saved were now in their late teens to early twenties and were now dating, going off to college, getting married, and starting their own families. It had been fourteen years, after all. Others had grown up and decided that they were done with going to church, and were off trying to "find" themselves. Here I was coming out of the fog and trying to find my place again. I also didn't meet anyone at that conference, and that really bothered me.

As I headed home after the conference, I felt like I was giving myself another reality check. I trusted God. I have waited on God all of these years, but nothing had panned out the way I thought it would. I was not a missionary in Africa or anywhere. My biological clock was ticking very quickly away, and I was still single. I couldn't comprehend still being single after all these years. *What was wrong?* I thought to myself. *I'm relatively in shape, intelligent, committed to my relationship with Christ . . . why would that not be attractive to a godly man?* In fact, what made this even more puzzling was that through the years, I had been around a ton of single men, but it was like I was invisible. Other single women around me would be noticed.

My roommate at the time, who herself had been single for many years, told me after the conference, "It's like you have an invisibility cloak on." I laughed at her comment, but in some ways, it felt true. You can't date anyone if no one is interested in dating you. Over the years, many people would comment that I wasn't in places where I could meet anyone. But the fact of the matter was prior to being sick, and especially as a single person, I used to travel quite a bit. Probably more than anyone that had made comments realized. I have had the opportunity to meet people everywhere. Multiple conferences year after year in Texas, Arizona, and Massachusetts. Besides church conferences, I had gone with outreach teams in various places including Toronto, Montreal, Washington State, Oregon, Virginia, Florida, Puerto Rico, Pennsylvania, New Jersey, New York, and Connecticut. I had also traveled for vacations, hitting places like Alaska, Chicago, Atlanta, and the Cayman Islands. I had an outgoing personality which was a far cry from my withdrawn, OCD past. It presented many opportunities for me to meet people, so clearly, that wasn't the issue.

I thought about how I constantly fended off questions from my family of when I would get married—"What was I waiting on?" Coworkers and strangers would constantly ask, "So when are you going to get married? What are you waiting on? Does he have to go to your church? Have you thought of a dating site?" People at church, who years ago agreed it was a fantastic idea to just wait on God, were now asking questions like, "So don't you want to get married?" The issue of standards came up often. My dad told me I would have to be willing to accept certain things. What if the guy doesn't have a job because he fell on hard times? I cannot have unattainable standards. Even though I had certain expectations, I cannot date if no one expresses an interest to date. Am I supposed to throw myself at a random stranger?

Chapter 11

The Pages Will Turn

As years of singleness continued, I did what I knew to do: I prayed, read my Bible, stayed involved in church, and I lived. There were times that the struggle was real as I could feel the weight of the perceived pause in my life. There were days that I felt consumed by my emotions. On these days, I brought myself back before God and affirmed His promises and His Word in my life. I knew that God was real. His evidence was all around me.

During this period, I had an injury to my right foot. For months I had pain around the ball of my foot, specifically in the pads under the toe bones. This continued for a long time until eventually I woke up one morning to go to work and I was unable to put my foot down on the floor to get out of bed. The pain was excruciating, and my foot was inflamed. I went to see a podiatrist who happened to be attending our church at the time. He examined my foot and determined I had symptoms consistent with metatarsalgia, which is a condition causing inflammation and swelling around the ball of the foot. I was given crutches to get the pressure off of my foot and help the swelling while we determined what the next steps would be in treating it.

Two weeks after I was given crutches, I went to the midweek service at church. There was a guest preacher in the service that evening. At the conclusion of the service, the pastor asked me if he could pray for me. He asked what was wrong with my foot. The podiatrist who was in the service that evening spoke up, explaining what the issue was. After the pastor prayed for me, he asked me to do something I was not able to do. I was not able to bear any weight on my foot as the pain in my foot was excruciating. I immediately put my foot down and was able to put weight on it. Not only was I able to put weight on the foot, I started first walking, then jogging. No pain at all. After months of being in pain, I was free of pain. It was a genuine miracle, witnessed by everyone at church including the podiatrist. This wasn't an act or a magic trick. I was completely healed.

The next morning, I woke up early and went running. My foot felt great. I knew that God answered prayers. Somewhere in the back of my mind, I thought, *Well, if God can heal my foot than certainly He can bring someone into my life. So why the wait?* There must be something more to this. As the year came to a close, I prayed that I would stay committed to my relationship with God. A few months after the incident with my foot, I decided to visit my sister and her family in San Antonio. It was the beginning of the new year, and I was excited for the break. My sister joined the military about a year after I did and had decided to reenlist after her obligatory service. At this point, she had been in the Navy for

The Pages Will Turn

about eighteen years, having recently returned from a tour in Afghanistan. A few days into my visit, I got up early to pray and spend some time with God before church that morning. I was praying a verse that had come to mind. I opened my Bible and began to read a passage in the Old Testament.

"For the Lord your God is bringing you into a good land, a land of brooks of water, of fountains and springs, flowing out in the valleys and hills, a land of wheat and barley, of vines and fig trees and pomegranates, a land of olive trees and honey, a land in which you will eat bread without scarcity, in which you will lack nothing, a land whose stones are iron, and out of whose hills you can dig copper. And you shall eat and be full, and you shall bless the Lord your God for the good land he has given you.

"Take care lest you forget the Lord your God by not keeping his commandments and his rules and his statutes, which I command you today, lest, when you have eaten and are full and have built good houses and live in them, and when your herds and flocks multiply and your silver and gold is multiplied and all that you have is multiplied, then your heart be lifted up, and you forget the Lord your God, who brought you out of the land of Egypt, out of the house of slavery, who led you through the great and terrifying wilderness, with its fiery serpents and scorpions and thirsty ground where there was no water, who brought you water out of the flinty rock, who fed you in the wilderness with manna that your fathers did not know, that he might humble you and test you, to do you good in the end. Beware lest you say in your heart, 'My power and the might of my hand have gotten me this wealth'" (Deuteronomy 8:7-17, ESV).

As I began reading, it was like the words were alive, breathing, and speaking right to my heart. I knew at the moment the page in my life was going to turn. It was like in a moment of time what I can only describe as the "pause button" I had felt for so long shifted to "play." I knew God was going to do something big.

That morning I went to church with a friend I knew from one of our churches in San Antonio. She has since gone on to be with the Lord. Doris was a good friend, born in Rhode Island, joining the Air Force, where she ended up eventually being stationed in San Antonio. Doris had become a Christian after coming out of a life of homosexuality. Doris' life exemplified what it was to live for Jesus. She shared what God did in her life to anyone who would listen. Life had not been easy for her. Doris' first husband had died a few years after they had gotten married, and she stayed single for almost sixteen years, just serving God. She had an infectious personality, just full of life and excitement even through illness and cancer that would eventually take her life. She had recently gotten married at the time of my visit to my sister and was so ecstatic as God had literally brought her husband to her, after waiting so long.

Doris would often stay with my roommate and me when she came to visit her family in Rhode Island and would always encourage us to just wait on God. That Sunday on our way to church Doris and I talked catching up on life. The worship service was great, and I was excited to hear the pastor's sermon. As he got up to preach, to my absolute surprise, he asked everyone to turn to the book of Deuteronomy 8. Verse 7. The exact scripture I had read earlier! As he began to read, I didn't know whether to laugh or cry! I was stunned.

I began to hear that small voice speaking to my heart that yes, the page was going to turn, and I need to not forget what God has brought me through. It was very humbling and at the same time vindicating. I felt like I had emerged from the desert. God was in control, and He knew exactly the "whys", "when," and "how" over the last ten years. As I returned home, I thought about this for weeks. I thought for sure that I was going to meet my husband-to-be any day now. But as the months passed, I sort of forgot about it until one afternoon in October . . . but it was not a husband-to-be.

The day started like any other. I was up early for work but somehow frantically running out the door on the verge of being late. While at work, I was mentally preparing myself to leave that evening for the conference at the church on the Cape. I was not going to be able to attend the entire conference, but I would be able to drive there after work to catch the evening services. As my workday was ending, I received a phone call from Belen (MaB as I now affectionately called her). She told me that she had almost forgotten to tell me this, but she wanted to tell me right away as the deadline was the next day. She had received an email from an adoption agency in Texas that was reaching out to families to host a child from China with special needs for six weeks in December, and she thought of me.

It would be noble to say my first reaction was a yes. But the reality was, it was so unexpected that my initial reaction was one of a deflection. I told her that I didn't think I'm in any position right now to host a child. MaB went on to explain that apparently, the agency offers a hosting program twice a year. I told her that I don't think right now is the best time for me. I was having work done on my house, and at the same time I was working on trying to get out of the debt I had accumulated over the years. Although I babysat here and there, I didn't think I could handle a child for that long. Besides, I was working full time. What would I do about childcare? I thought these were solid, valid excuses, but MaB was persistent. She asked me what I was waiting on, to which I repeated my reasons. I also added that I would look into it the next time the hosting opportunity came up. Instead of just saying, "Okay," she proceeded to tell me: "Well, you get into debt for stupid things—why not for something more valuable?"

As tough as this might be perceived, I had spoken often about adopting an older special-needs child, so when the opportunity came up to host a little one for the holidays, she thought of me—but I had envisioned things a different way. She did have a point. I absolutely loved shopping and didn't bat an eye paying big money on expensive clothes and shoes. How difficult could this be? I told MaB I thought about what she said, and I would do it. I contacted the agency in Texas and within a week's time, I began the process of applying and getting approved to host a little boy from China (who would eventually become my son). The weeks before his arrival in December were like a whirlwind of applications, background checks, shopping for clothes, outfitting a room, and getting books and some toys. Before I knew it, I was standing in line at JFK airport in New York awaiting his arrival. When the group of children came out of the customs area with their sponsors to meet the small group of host parents, it was pretty overwhelming and a bit chaotic. We were all soon matched with our host child, and I met the rambunctious little boy that I would be a parent to for six weeks.

I was struck by how small he was for an eight-year old. He looked about four years old, but looks can be deceiving. He was so mischievous and practically broke everything in my non-childproof home whenever I wasn't looking. A few days after his arrival, I received a call from the adoption agency informing me that the rules for single-parent adopting were changing at the beginning of the year, which was two weeks away. They informed me that if I wanted to adopt the little one I was hosting, I would have to decide *that day*. I didn't even have time to be surprised. In hindsight, I realized that God knows us so well and has a way of doing things.

Being an analyst, I probably would have spent days, maybe even weeks, pondering this decision to adopt a child from every angle possible. But I didn't even have the time to think about this because if I didn't act, the opportunity would be gone. I told the woman on the other end of the phone that I would go forward with adopting. After six weeks of hosting the children, they all had to go back to China before I could officially adopt him. Sending my little guy back on the plane was one of the hardest things I have ever done in my life. He was so small, so helpless, without a family and without love in that orphanage. I could hardly bear it.

It would be two years before I laid eyes on him again, this time in China. The road to adoption was long, very difficult, and at times almost impossible. As life would have it, I obviously never imagined that I would become a single mom, and that was part of the hesitation initially. I remember one day many years ago, over coffee telling, MaB and my roommate that I really felt like God had put it in my heart to adopt and specifically from China. It was just a desire I had in my heart, but I never pursued it or thought about it much after that. I figured I would get married one day and look into adoption when the time seemed right. I couldn't even grasp fully that I was about to become a parent of not just one child, but two. Yes, two! Along with the processing of adopting my son, I stumbled upon a picture of a little girl in a very poor city in China who was up for adoption. I felt drawn to her but also scared of her at the same time. She appeared to have some pretty significant developmental delays. Even though the couple videos sent were less than five minutes long, I could see in one of them her struggle to put on a sweater and sneakers. And in the other, her struggle to verbally communicate, hold a crayon as they had her at a table with a coloring book, and she seemed to be not mentally present. She was really disconnected as the people in the video spoke to her. I wasn't sure if I would be able to handle the level of delays. I decided to pray, and in the end, I felt strongly that it was something God wanted me to do.

Everything that could possibly go wrong in an adoption process went wrong. Misinformation, mistakes with the reports and filings, being lied to, being initially denied the adoption of one of the children because of my race, constant staff turnover at the adoption agency—Satan threw everything he had at me. There were times I was just exhausted with the whole process and would just cry. But God proved faithful, and almost two years later, all of the finances came through for the adoption of the two children and the approval to bring them home together came a day before my thirty-eighth birthday. Four months later, I was on a plane to China, and just like that, I became a mom to two beautiful children. Even through all of the setbacks, in a strange sort of way, I had grown accustomed to waiting. The subject of marriage couldn't be escaped even in China. During one of the processing days, I was being interviewed by an officer processing the adoption of my daughter. I was a bit nervous waiting for my turn to be interviewed. As I sat across from the officer, he began to ask me why I wanted to adopt my daughter. He gestured several times with his hands, acting out that she was crazy to me, over and over again. He seemed perplexed as to why I would want to adopt a child with significant needs as hers. As we spoke, my daughter was busy flipping over the chairs in the office, appearing very wild as she groaned and mumbled to herself. At one point, the official looks at me and said, "So, when you get married one day, what do you plan to do with her? What if the person you are going to marry do not want her . . . what are you going to do?"

I looked at him and responded, "I will not marry anyone that does not want my daughter."

He looked at me incredulously and shook his head, and that was the end of that. I realized at that moment it's one thing to be single with no children, but it's another to be single with multiple children—and with significant needs. But what was I going to do? Let them stay and languish in an orphanage because I want to get married? I found that to be incredibly ridiculous and very limiting. As I headed back to the States with the children, I wondered what the future held for us. I didn't have a clue how to be a parent to these two children, but I really believed that God would help. He did not move in the impossible without a purpose in mind.

Chapter 12

Dealing with Loneliness

Parenting is a difficult job, and single parenting seems even more so. I never understood or considered what single parents have to deal with until I became one. The first year was somewhat of an understandable fog. The children's many needs were varied. It seemed like every time I turned around, I was discovering something else. Illnesses, unknown diseases, malnourishment, baby teeth falling out. Then unto puberty almost overnight, lack of language, and a range of emotions from confusion, anger, to defiance.

My daughter was like a large two-year-old, unable to eat without choking, unable to use the bathroom by herself, or walk unassisted. She began to have constant, serious skin infections. There were days I wondered if I could really do this. On top of this was the fight to keep my job. As the kids' needs were extreme, I could no longer work in the office full-time.

I had to split my days half in the office and half working at home in the evenings, into the night. I could not get the kids in school because of their lack of prior education.

I had a nine and ten-year-old who did not even have kindergarten-level education in China due to their significant needs. The school district where we lived had no idea how to meet their needs and insisted that they be placed in age-appropriate grade levels, which was, to be blunt, insane. I fought for placement and an individualized learning plan all the way up the food chain from the school to the superintendent's office to the Rhode Island education commissioner's office to no avail. It was like something out of a movie.

As I struggled through all of this, the comments and observations came in full force. I had people telling me "That's why you shouldn't have become a single parent! Who does that?" or "How could struggling this badly be God?" "God did not intend for people to be a single parent," or even, "You did everything backwards. Aren't you supposed to marry than have children?"

Through it all, I prayed. I prayed that God would give me wisdom in dealing with my situation, and I prayed that God would give me strength. If there was anything that I had learned over the years, it was that God moves in the impossible. In Mark 10, we read, "Jesus looked at them and said, 'with man it is impossible, but not with God. For all things are possible with God'" (Mark 10:27, ESV). My situation seemed impossible, but I knew God would work things through.

About a year after the children were home, I decided to give up fighting with the school system in Rhode Island as I was getting nowhere. The school district where we lived finally decided to out-district the children, but this was useless as no other school district in the surrounding cities would pick them up. District after district informed me that they were not equipped to deal with the needs of my children. I realized there was nothing more I could do. My mom, who lived in Boston, reached out to someone she knew in the Boston school district and they were able to place the kids in a school.

I moved in temporarily with one of my cousins. The kids and I stayed at her house during the week, coming back to Rhode Island on the weekends. After putting the kids on the bus each morning, I would commute almost an hour to two some days back to Rhode Island for work and church. I spent a year doing this until I found a school system in another city in Massachusetts that was willing to work with me regarding the children's education needs.

After a couple of months of apartment hunting, we finally found a place to live, and I put my house up for sale. Leaving Rhode Island felt very strange. It had been my beloved home for the past twenty years. Even though I had only owned my home for five years, there were a lot of memories I was leaving behind. The home provided employment for some as I had a lot of work done on the house. It became home to my roommates' mom in the last year of her life. There were many fellowships with friends and church family as well as holiday celebrations with my own family. It was in this home that I finally graduated college, hosted a little boy who would eventually become my son, and now was home to both of my children. All of these memories flooded back as I packed up the house. I began to pray as I often did on my back porch. I knew that God could do anything, so why not just work out the situation here?

I also knew these precious kids were God's gift to me. With everything I had gone through in the adoption process, it was simply a miracle that these children were here. I was not looking to adopt or even thinking of children at the time. I was just living and seeking God to turn the page in my life, and He did, but not in the way I thought. And although I was deeply grateful and humbled by this, I wondered wouldn't it have made more sense to be married and start a family than being a single mom? Why not send a husband after all of these years? And as clear as day, I felt God speaking to me that this was His plan.

Now, I wish I could say my next thought was one of acceptance. Instead, I literally said out loud, "No way!"

God's plan was for me to be single all these years? I became a Christian at twenty-one years old. I was now in my forties! This just can't be God's plan. But as I spoke it, I knew right then and there that it was. But I just couldn't believe it. What purpose did this serve? I asked myself over and over again. Why would God want me to do this alone? Wouldn't it make more sense to have a helper? Someone to fight along with me! As I mulled all of these questions in my head, I thought back to a previous conversation I had one night after church with my old roommate and MaB. They really challenged my thinking as I had become so engulfed in my situation with the kids that I was leaving God out of the picture. My shoulders were heavy with the constant battle of the schools, my job situation, endless commuting. What happened to trusting God and getting Him involved in my situation? I needed the wake-up call because it is very easy to be consumed in your problems that you don't see what God was doing.

As I settled into my new apartment with the children, about a month in, I began to feel a sense of loneliness that I had never experienced. It was strange. Although I lived as a single person all these years, I really never felt lonely. The kids were in two different schools across the city, and the meeting with the schools seemed endless. Added to this was the ongoing, many doctor appointments. Moving to the Boston area meant the new issue of heavy traffic for an appointment. A ten-mile drive was about an hour on average.

We continued to attend church in Rhode Island, so the mid-week service run was at times a two-hour commute to the church prior to the 2019 pandemic, COVID, which carried into several more years. I would get home at night exhausted with barely enough energy to get up early and get out of the house the next morning. As this continued for months, the weight of my responsibilities and loneliness felt heavier and heavier. I would cry out to God daily, but things got even harder. I felt as if I could not accept that this was God's plan for me and my children.

One afternoon, almost a year after our move, I reached my breaking point. I had started a new job as a senior insurance underwriter at a company in Boston, but the commute was even more difficult than commuting to Rhode Island every day. I was still in training for the position a month in. While at work, my boss called me on the phone and stated that she needed to speak with me the next day as it appeared that I did not appreciate the training I was getting. I told her that I did appreciate the training, but I was eager to get started at my job after almost a month of being there. The truth was the training was too much. I came from an assistant vice president position at my last job, and I did not need my hand held. I had been doing my job for a very long time and I could figure things out on my own. I actually learned better that way.

As I hung up the phone with her, I realized that I was done. I packed my desk up and quit my job. I decided to stay home with my kids. I was beginning to feel disconnected from the kids as I was just simply exhausted, and I knew I needed to find God in my situation. It may not have been the wisest thing to do. I didn't have a plan. I had managed to save a few months of my salary, and I decided that I was going to stay home and focus on my kids. And I did.

    Six months later, I accepted a position working at home for a tech company. Going back to school for technology came in handy all of these years later. I was able to work while being there for my children. God had proven faithful even when I was not. Having a spouse did not make these things work out but trusting and relying on God when our situation seem dire. All too often I have heard women say over the years, "Well, if I had a husband than I wouldn't have to deal with this or that." I said it myself! But the reality is even with a spouse your situation at home, with the kids, finances, and health, it can all seem to spin out of control. And it is God who meets our needs and ministers to our weary souls in our times of great need.

Chapter 13

Understanding God's Plan

Surrendering wasn't easy for me. During the time I was home, I began to seek God. And by seeking God, I prayed, I read my Bible, I went to church, and I spent time with my kids. Every day, I made it a point to do these things, and it's not that I hadn't done these things before, but sometimes in the busyness of life we just check our little boxes in our walk with God.

"Okay, I said a prayer today, check! I read my bible, check!"

In these things that seem so basic, this is where you find God. A relationship has to be cultivated and guarded. I was carrying all of life's burdens on my own, and it was *exhausting*. In 1 Peter 5:7 (ESV), it reads "casting all your anxieties on him because he cares for you." Becoming spun out in life can be our undoing, but coming back to the place where we are God-focused is a choice. It takes a decision, and I had to make that decision. I realized that God has a plan for each individual's life. More often than not, it doesn't and will never line up with our plans, desires, and wants. Why would singleness for all of these years be God's plan? I may never fully understand it.

During the process of adoption, the life and background of potential parents are examined in detail. A single parent is scrutinized even more. The stability of a job, your finances, educational background, and ability to provide a stable and loving home are all considered. All these things came to me through the years and paved the way for me to become a mom. So perhaps the wait was never about me but about the children and God's greater plan.

I came to the place where I accepted the wait, and it brought a relief, joy, and peace to my heart. Proverbs 16:8 (ESV) says "The heart of man plans his way, but the Lord establishes his steps." Sometimes the wait isn't because of anything you have done, should have done, or could have done. Sometimes it's simply for God's reasoning, plans, and purposes. Deuteronomy 8:2, NKJV says, "And you shall remember that the Lord your God led you all the way these forty years in the wilderness, to humble you and test you, to know what was in your heart, whether you would keep his commandments or not."

It's very easy to proclaim all of what we will do for God or say what we would never do. I have learned over the years who we really are and what we are made of with regards to convictions and our heart comes out over time. God could have simply brought Israel out of Egypt and out of the hands of Pharaoh overnight, in a blink of an eye. However, through forty years, God chose to bring them through the process of deliverance and did it in the most spectacular way imaginable—literally separating the sea so they can walk through on dry land to the other side.

Over the years, I have been impatient, frustrated, angry, passive, dismissive, discontented, repentant, contented, patient, surrendered, but yet I've waited. God doesn't take away the intensity of desire, of feeling alone, the innate part of us that wants companionship. But He has given us Himself, the fulfillment of all of our needs. All of our innermost needs and desires will never be met by another human being as much as we think it will. If you cannot be content in Christ, you will still be searching even if someone does come along.

While you wait, you need to live. Life doesn't begin and end with a spouse. There will be so much of life missed if life is lived in that manner. In a world where there is always a way or an "art" of doing something, I have found that in waiting, there isn't some manipulation involved. It is just simply surrendering to God's sovereignty, a willingness to obey, and a heart that desires to do what is right, despite what we see. Our emotions and desires, as overwhelming as they might seem at times, must be surrendered to Him. There is contentment that must be found in Jesus, the source of who we are and what we do. One of my favorite verses, Ephesians 3:2 (NKJV), says "... Now to him who is able to do exceedingly abundantly above all that we ask or think, according to the power that works in us, to him be glory in the church by Christ Jesus to all generations, forever and ever. Amen."

No one said being a Christian would be easy. We may never fully understand why things happen the way they do, but it doesn't mean God doesn't see. It doesn't mean that He is not faithful. When I became a Christian over twenty years ago, I made a promise to God that I would live my life for Him no matter what. I had no idea at the time what that meant. How shallow of me to throw in the towel, so to speak, because things don't go the way I imagined that they would! Why do things have to go the way I think they should? A relationship with God is not solely based on what our eyes see. Hebrews 11:1 (NKJV) says, "Now faith is the substance of things hoped for, the evidence of things not seen." Just as it takes faith to believe that God will move in our impossible situations, it takes faith to put our lives fully in His hands, for His purposes. Those purposes can include marriage or being single. Perhaps being a pastor or pastor's wife, missionary, or maybe in your profession. Whatever it may be, our lives must be lived for and in Christ.

Will I ever get married? I have been told over the years that God will bring this man into my life. I know that God is faithful to keep His promises, but whether it happens or not, it does not change my relationship with God. The longer that I have been a Christian the more precious my relationship to God has become as I realize a lot more is at stake. We affect a lot of people in our life along the journey of life and it's not always in a good way. But with Christ, we can find fulfillment and purpose and affect those around us for Him.

To God be the glory!

www.ingramcontent.com/pod-product-compliance
Lightning Source LLC
LaVergne TN
LVHW051708080426
835511LV00017B/2791